MW01114808

TALKING
TO A TREE

HEAP OF STONES

TALKING TO A TREE

Poems of a Fragile World

AE BALLAKISTEN

Talking to a Tree

by AE Ballakisten

First published by Theart Press in 2011

Copyright © AE Ballakisten

www.aeballakisten.com

ISBN: 978-0-620-51066-0

Front cover painting by Warwick Goldswain

Set in Adobe Jensen Pro and Fontin Sans

Page design and typesetting by Mousehand

Dedicated to

NELSON ROLIHLAHLA MANDELA

CONTENTS

PART ONE

MY ERA 3

UNCLE JOHN 4

SHREDDERS 6

FLIGHTLESS BIRDS 8

THE GENTLE ART OF TERRORISM 10

OBAMA, OSAMA, OH MAMA! 12

MISSION OF THE GUN 13

LETTER TO THE OTHER SIDE 14

THE LAW OF THE SAVAGE 15

MARX'S LIONS 17

PARABOLA 18

PART TWO

KITTEN 25

THE TAKING OF THERESSA 26

GIANT TIN CAN 28

BEGGARS 30

ONE BRIGHT AUGUST DAY 33

MAN OR DRONE? 35

SEEING ANGELINA NAKED 39

ON BEAUTY 40

ON GOOD AND BAD 41

MORE   43

BUSINESSMAN OF THE YEAR   45

MODERN ART   46

PART THREE

WORLD PEACE   51

TALKING TO A TREE   52

ONLY THE LISTENING   53

MAN'S SALVATION   54

SILLY QUESTION   55

AFTER FREEDOM   56

BREAKFAST, 22 DECEMBER 2012   57

ROLIHLAHLA   59

ABOUT THE AUTHOR   62

PART ONE

We are continually being urged by our training and traditions to antagonisms and conflicts that will impoverish, starve and destroy both our antagonists and ourselves.

H.G. WELLS

Led by the ignorant and mad, we live in worlds … where bombs are good, and people bad.

JAMES KIRKUP

Patriotism is not enough. I must have no hatred or bitterness for anyone.

EDITH CAVELL

MY ERA

we have so much yet

everywhere

mothers

cry

we know so much yet

daily

so many people

die

seems the

more

we have and the

more

we know the

more

we need to

lie

UNCLE JOHN

They fought against Midian, as the Lord commanded Moses, and killed every man. Moses said, "Now kill all the boys. And kill every woman …"
                            THE BIBLE, NUMBERS 31

"We have always been killing each other,"
Uncle John replied, calmly, matter-of-factly
with a hint of "don't come here to preach
your new-age leftist naïve shit." *Always?*
"Khoikhoi killing San
Vikings killing Irish
Romans killing English
English killing Boers." *But thou shalt*
not kill, Uncle John, "Germans
killing Polish
Japanese killing Chinese
Americans killing Iraqis." *But thou shalt*
not kill, Uncle John. "Israelites
killing Midianites!" he continued, measured
another length of wood, sawed and
nailed to craft a rectangular wooden box
in which a boy would take his place
alongside mankind to fulfil his destiny.
"We have always been killing each other,
so who are you

to say that we should stop

when it is what we have always been doing

led by kings, by popes, by God!"

Uncle John was clearly possessed by the devil

so I killed him.

SHREDDERS

We had all seen the enormous shed
set against a dark, misty mountain,
but no-one talked about it –
forbidden to mention it. A rickety shed,
desperately holding onto its walls
as if a hiccup could take it to its ankles.
Inside, a yellow light
waved around causing
shadows to frog-jump all over the inner walls;
hints of this drama flickered through the slits
in the doors and the walls;
a high-pitch grinding stabbed from the shed,
like a butcher's electric blade through bone;
a perpetual high pitch grinding in that rickety shed
with leaping shadows peeking through slits.

We weren't allowed to go there –
we were soldiers, men. Girls,
and communists went into the shed
but not God's men, king's men,
heroes. Instead
we gouged out our consciences,
we killed for life
waged war for peace

wiped out Germans and French and Americans, British
and Iraqis and Libyans, Palestinians and Afghanistanis.

And then one day I weakened
and went into the shed. Inside,
vast machines,
spewing out thin stringy strips of paper.
Shredders!
At one end of the room, gigantic heaps of books
    and documents,
(bibles, korans, toras and constitutions of warring nations)
at the other end, a little mound
of thin stringy strips of paper. "For every death,
we shred a book and a constitution," explained the foreman,
a condemned frail man
with a ten thousand year old face
and wintry eyes,
"but the mound of shredded paper is so small," I replied.
And then he slowly pointed, out the back
I saw a mountain of rotting souls
heaped upon our vacant gouged-out consciences
and a planet of shredded paper. "Bluddy girls
and communists," I thought, and
returned to the front line.

FLIGHTLESS BIRDS

In a 3am haze
all you need is a tranquiliser,
some noise,
like a cross to fend off the nightmare demons,
noise to outnoise them,
so channel choice is random;
I settle on the most grey I can find:
two old scientists arguing over a new bird species
found in the deserts of Afghanistan;
sleep mist descends at pace,
I hear the nightmares walking toward me
from everywhere in the house,
but then a soldier,
a man in military uniform enters.
The mist lifts and the nightmares retreat, disappointed.
I can feel the fear in the air
of which the military man speaks.
My toes dig into the hot yellow desert sand,
digging into death.
Tranced by his memories
(seems he too could do with a tranquiliser,
perhaps this explains his presence)
"Why do those desert vultures not fly?"
he is asked impatiently.

"Because of the war."

The words seem to flow out of his soul, reluctantly,

    like thick, viscous sludge,

like they too are afraid of this century.

"Ample food in the desert.

Wings too weak to carry their stuffed bellies.

Disuse has made their wings forget."

The older scientist vomits.

The soldier allows tears.

Then thundering chaos

as I get ambushed and suffocated

by bold returning nightmares.

THE GENTLE ART OF TERRORISM

little mike and his little friend burt
are watching another episode of
"Dog and Cat"

Cat has a soft toy that Dog wants
but Cat will not give it to Dog,
so Dog doesn't like Cat.
Dog could just snatch the toy
but then Dog would seem like a bad dog amongst his friends
and his puppies would not respect him;
so Dog devises a plan –
he accuses Cat of being a puppy-killer
(a ludicrous accusation – do cats really kill puppies?)
Waves of shock shriek all around the animal kingdom;
other cats are horrified (though some secretly wish it was true),
dogs are incensed as
evidence is broadcast of the puppy killings and the cute little
    puppies lying dead
(the kids find this most hilarious.)
With cat-hatred at an all-time high,
everywhere dogs start assaulting cats,
and Dog leads an assault on Cat with the support of every dog
    in the kingdom
until Cat and his friends and family are killed

and cats everywhere are persecuted –
all for a soft toy!
Dog happily swoops in and grabs Cat's toy
and plays with it all day
and shows it off to all dogs and cats
to remind them of his greatness.

little abdul and his little friend mohammed
are also watching.

OBAMA, OSAMA, OH MAMA!

obama, osama, oh mama!
this is not a comedy, nor a drama
identical faces, they must be twins
identical characters, identical sins

they both are mad, both insane
both breathe death like a hurricane
puppets of hatred on a global stage
stuffing man into a shrinking cage

both are wrong, believing they're right
(blind belief always turns day to night)
once men of God with eyes turned high
now truth forgotten, living Satan's lie

not a comedy mama, nor is this a drama
man's worst horror, this obama, osama
war, shuts heaven's door, they must see,
buries God with brother, setting Satan free

MISSION OF THE GUN

I have been well trained, I've been taught
Success must be earned, can't be bought
Without sharp focus, acts yield naught

So I do not dance, do not sing
Your burger and chips, I will not bring
I don't read books or any such thing

My purpose in life, aim to fill
With perfection and utmost skill
Is not to give life, but to kill

LETTER TO THE OTHER SIDE

Our God calls *us* to be patriotic
to defend our heritage
to honour our forefathers
to secure our way of life
to take care of our families.

So we make pre-emptive strikes.

Wouldn't you
if you were us?

THE LAW OF THE SAVAGE

Part I

Clarence Humphries was a magnificently
handsome man; the perfection of his physique
and manly manliness only outdone by
his colossal intellect. He strut with a
brilliant arrogance. His wrought-iron square jaw and
battleship chest barged through the insecurities
of crowds and friends and those idiotic enough
to linger. He hovered above the ordinary,
mastered the never-achieved, the undone
and unsaid; he commanded a presence that
compelled men to bow, women to faint, until

Part II

Frank Fletcher swung an angry uncivilised
uncultured fist, the size of Scotland, into
his face, and shattered his jaw, buckled his nose,
ripped the cheeks from his cheekbones, plucked the lashes
from his lids, detoothed his gums and flattened him
right in front of his manor house in Surrey.
Clarence Humphries became spectacularly
unhandsome, supremely unattractive; the
pinnacle of human deformation. And
word spread that Humphries got Fletchered. And Fletcher

became feared and respected, and became a
fantastically famous man, and revered;
his company sought, his famous fist pictured
and bronzed and printed on T-shirts, and he strut
with a brilliant arrogance, invincible,
this hero, giant man with his dinosaur
powers and bone-crushing mammoth fist, until

Part III

the savages came and devoured him. A
charging army of flesh-hungry savages,
hungry from neglect and non-maintenance came
and devoured him, and Clarence and all those
who hated Clarence and all those who feared Frank
and all those who saw no difference between
Clarence and Frank. Brutally rapidly gone.
In a violent bloody flash. Devoured. Gone.

MARX'S LIONS

Observe the lion
When he has the comfort of his prey-filled territory
And ample trees for shade
And a watering hole close by
And a pride with young females
He will defend his territory with his life.

Observe a second lion
He is unhappy with his barren territory
The terrain is flat, scorched desert
And his pride has withered
Nothing can keep him from exploring and pursuing a better life.

Isolated, natural behaviour
Until the first lion has what the second lion needs.

PARABOLA

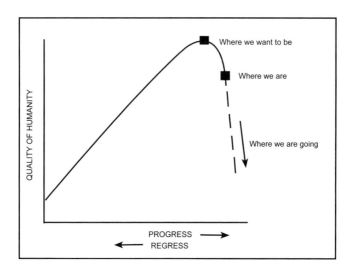

Policemen found him,

the old mad bum;

he was badly beaten,

beaten by governments, by corporations

by blind men.

In one hand, a bottle of rum, in the other,

a crumpled, blood-stained sheet of paper –

a parabola drawn on it.

He mumbled incoherent gibberish

"return to the ocean

to the tree

to man

to God

to be more

to be;

they would not listen."

The policemen laughed

and went on their way.

Later that night

Jesus wept.

PART TWO

... the only comfort that my mind could find to say
was, that God, who makes tomorrow makes it better than today.

JOHN MASEFIELD

KITTEN

Still
she lies,
her pure-white, soft coat
like a fist
wearing a white cashmere glove,
tucked between a fluffy cushion
and the huge arm
of the sofa. Not dead,
still –
her breathing is visible
like the rhythm of waves
of a deep dark blue sea;
peaceful,
like she's just had a saucer of milk
or a rough play session
with that doll she enjoys
peaceful
until the next time.

THE TAKING OF THERESSA

She'd been violated before. Men
with sin on their minds. She
salivating for love. So Theressa came to know
sin, man's sin, and love was forgotten
in the effluent that would be flung
onto her belly, or inside her thigh, or in her face
which would dry and become crusted. Hope of love
caught in a vortex of sin and desire and trust
earning her the reputation of 'easy'. Ultimately
she too was a sinner, guilty of seeking angels
in Satan's den.

But then why was she now so more
disturbed? Why did she feel so more
violated, more
taken?

This man,
revolting in his masculinity, blatant
and brash, a sewer creature, a swamp nigger, face of a
stillborn baby, hair like serrated womb-scrapers, body
like a black wall against which rape victims are lined up to have
their pictures taken. What was he doing in her bedroom?
His stench

burned her nostrils. His breath evoked spasms of nausea.

As he grabbed her,

silent tears streamed down her cheeks. Her skin

shuddered as his coarse hard razor flesh touched hers. Drawn

so close to him that she could feel her heartbeat vibrating off his

chest. Caged in his cold steel arms she

clenched her jaw, her fist, her groin; not to keep him

out, just to put up *that* fight, that fight

to preserve some dignity. He breathed into her hair, took deep

gutteral breaths into her neck, wheezed onto her

naked shoulders. Standing there, trapped, she

could feel his thick erect penis press against her belly.

With his rat-like eyes closed he

smelled her,

inhaled her,

consumed her all-over-inside-outside scent –

mango, Chanel, the Lagavulin

between her thighs. Something inside her

collapsed. And then

he was gone.

GIANT TIN CAN

A giant tin can stood
in the middle of our village;
a huge old oil tank perhaps
that dominated the skyline;
it was the size of many men
standing on each other's shoulders, and
as wide as an elephant herd; chickens
wandered around it, pecking
at invisible edibles in the sand, children
too were drawn to it, using it
as a backboard for children's games; old men
leaned against the giant tin can
while chewing on a stick of wood
or tobacco. Large and dominant
this vast black can, like
a storm cloud that hovers
eternally; rusted and rotten,
dented and bashed
with holes stabbed all over it –
small piercings and large holes
the size of a man's heart.

Father told me that
the giant tin can

was once magnificent, that

it had once shone like the noon sun, and

that every day, men

and women, young

and old, and children

climbed the ladder to the top of

the giant tin can; that

most of the time

it overflowed.

Father also told me

that God had put the

giant tin can

there, for us

to store up

all our hopes.

BEGGARS

Each day I stood

at the same traffic light –

corner of Rivonia and Outspan roads

begging,

for scraps,

for coins,

for mercy,

from those in BMWs and Jaguars and Audis

with a crumpled cardboard sign

"Please help. No food. No job"

I'd bend my knee

till it struck the earth,

cushioned by the hard, jagged asphalt,

my head bowed humbly,

my face pitiful.

I'd wave the royal beggar wave

like an idiot

as fumes from five-litre engines

filled my stomach.

The crumpled cardboard sign in my heart read

"Please help. No hope. No dignity"

for I'd dissolved a long time ago.

The faces in the cars would ignore me,

awkwardly, they'd turn their faces

away from me,

away from their shame

and wave a dismissive hand,

"Fuck off,

go get a job!"

I'd been offered a job

but I didn't want it;

I'd rather stand there.

The faces were right,

I should fuck off

because I didn't have to be there.

So I would be a beggar

and be ignored

and be sworn at

and get saliva-soaked leftover sandwiches

or a cigarette butt

or pneumonia.

Then one day

I took that job,

abandoned my corner – relief on the faces

in the BMWs and Jaguars and Audis.

But I still see those faces,

only now they don't ignore me;

waving, pleading, bowing, bending
begging,
only now it's not me –
"Please take whatever you want
just please don't hurt us,"
they beg.
We're actually all the same,
beggars;
it just depends on who's holding the money,
and who's holding the gun.
"Fuck off," I say,
"this is my job!"

ONE BRIGHT AUGUST DAY

George cried every day;

every day,

while he had hope.

Six years ago he stopped

crying, in that London basement

where he'd been blackened

and tried thirty times to stop his spirit.

One bright August day

George escaped. Blind,

he took brick to window,

any window, to return

the blackened hope

to that shapeless everywhere tormentor.

Mr and Mrs Posh watched the video,

with shock and bemusement,

of George hurling that brick,

"feral rat"

they called him

just before a policeman stood on his neck.

I HAVE NEVER BEEN

I CANNOT BE

George wrote on the wall of his cell

using his faeces.

Finally he got his wish;

this time,

his spirit stopped long enough

for him to be free.

Order restored,

and basement doors reinforced in their London home,

Mr and Mrs Posh returned to their thanksgiving

    prayers.

MAN OR DRONE?

Tick tock
Heartbeat

As I drive late at night
In a city that takes all
Like ants cleaning a bone
Tick tock
A body lying beneath a light
A drunk man who took a fall
For a pillow chose a stone?
Tick tock
Or discarded rags rolled up tight
And some bunched in a ball
To look like man's clone?
Tick tock
I keep driving till no sight
Of the man fallen in a brawl
And left in the road all alone
Tick tock
I make a u-turn to the right
If that's a man I make a call
To be a man and not a drone

Tick tock
Breath

Car parked, jacket tight

Darkness's dangers make me feel small

Exposed, with only a mobile phone

Tick tock

The cold rips like a terrier bite

The wind whips in squall

Just me and the black sky cone

Tick tock

And the heap, with my full might

I walk the fifty-metre haul

To this seed in heaven sown

Tick tock

What is his size or height

Round and fat or thin and tall

And named Jack or Joan?

Tick tock

My own fear shines bright

Demons in my head start to crawl

Have I put my life on loan?

Tick tock

I reach down into this plight

And poke this fallen Saul

Who to this spot was blown

Tick tock

No stir from the body despite

My shoving and pushing slight

"Boetie!" and a whistle tone

Tick tock

I get a godless fright

I shove against a hard cold wall

Is he dead, his spirit flown?

Tick tock

In shock, face bloodless white

I shake harder, I maul

And then some life, agonised moan

Tick tock

As though disturbing him out of spite

I see a black face wrapped in a shawl

Hello Saul or Jack, not Joan

Tick tock

Pride

I've done my duty, quite

The good citizen standing tall

Judged by a judge unknown

Tick tock

Others pass the light

Did I hurt him, cause the fall

With my car his body unsewn?

Tick tock

Surely they see this blight

And accuse me, dammitall

I'm a fool I should have known

Tick tock

I turn, to my car my flight

Risked danger to save this Saul

But this is not my cup not my zone

Tick tock

I race away, I leave the site

But did I touch that man at all

If my chaos has left him there alone?

Tick tock

Conscience

SEEING ANGELINA NAKED

I have not seen Angelina naked

or any famous woman with millions of fans

or any woman who appears in movies

or gyrates in sin in music videos

or spreads herself

across magazine covers.

Imagine the horror

of seeing such a person naked,

truly naked,

before the fake breasts or facial injections or nose work,

without the wig or false eyelashes

or the layer upon heap of chemicals and compounds with French
    names that,

make her less of a woman, so that

she can have confidence

to live a lie.

Actually … there'd be no horror,

how perfectly beautiful she would be.

ON BEAUTY

Sometimes the mask slips
and I can see her beauty.

৽

I will not wear any make-up today,
today I'd like to be beautiful.

৽

I have seen a beautiful man,
because I have seen a man.

৽

If your face is a lie
then how can there be truth
in anything you say or do.

৽

New research has found that
your appearance is just perfect,
contrary to media reports of the last 100 years.

ON GOOD AND BAD

Love and Hate

A heart that truly knows love cannot bear hatred for even just one man.

∾

It is impossible for a man to hate his neighbour yet love his brother. Hate and love cannot dwell in the same heart, either light overcomes darkness or darkness prevails.

Truth and Lies

It doesn't take great courage and leadership to send boys to battle, as some would have us believe; all it takes is a few simple lies.

∾

Man's awakening will occur when he rids himself of the lies that oppress him – the lies he tells himself and the lies of others that he chooses to believe.

∾

There are good people in bad places, and bad people in good places; sometimes it is difficult to know which is which.

Normal and Perverse

Victims create victims.

୬

It is a profound human tragedy, when in a society, human atrocities become the norm.

୬

Why are we surprised when a sick society produces sick people?

Peace and Violence

Violence begins where humanity ends.

୬

Peace-making is the steady process of converting enemies into friends.

୬

Like energy, enemies can only be transformed into another form, they can never be destroyed.

୬

Peace stays when greed goes.

MORE

I don't have enough
I want more
Three million or
Maybe even four

I don't have enough
I want more
Happiness will soar
Gold walls, gold floor

I don't have enough
I want more
Forbes in awe
I'm on Channel 4

I don't have enough
I want more
Economic whore
Exploit human flaw
Destroy competitor
I'll break the law
I'll start a war
Know what I'm fighting for

I don't have enough

I want more

Don't be a bore

Love is a chore

I don't have enough

I want more

My heart is sore

What, heaven's door?

My life I saw

My soul is raw

A rotten core

Please, no more!

BUSINESSMAN OF THE YEAR

Closer, closer
To total decay
The more I strive for that extra dollar

Closer, closer
To that extra dollar
The more I yield to total decay

MODERN ART

It made him vomit,

the series of paintings

(he was old,

from a gentler time)

of a woman shoving dollar bills up her vagina;

fisting herself to ensure a compact fit,

then masturbating

(some dollar bills still visible)

till she came.

The paintings were called

"Conception of Modern Man".

PART THREE

All of our humanity is dependent upon recognising the humanity in others.

DESMOND TUTU

For to be free is not merely to cast off one's chains, but to live in a way that respects and enhances the freedom of others.

NELSON MANDELA

WORLD PEACE

If I draw a circle
around me
and you draw a circle
around you,
then I am 'us'
and you are 'them'
and so we use all our strength and skill
and ingenuity and resources
to kill each other.

If we draw a circle
around both of us,
then we are brothers
and there is only 'us.'

TALKING TO A TREE

Hello tree,

majestic regal tree (with no name)

with your outstretched arms

and solemn face.

Silent

you have been for three hundred years

yet saying more

than all of mankind;

just being a tree

not flapping your branches

to be a bird

or hooving your roots in the plains

to be a wildebeest;

just standing here,

unmoved

in truth.

ONLY THE LISTENING

There is a destiny
that haunts you, in the dark
of your meandering.
Only the listening
see
the tiny luminous pebbles
that lead to the light.
In that light,
a choir,
singing the eternal song
but deformed of one voice;
on cue
you come to life,
but only if you've been listening.

MAN'S SALVATION

We all take –
The strong take whatever they want
The weak take whatever is left
The strong take from the weak
The weak take their revenge;
And so man withers.

If we all give –
The strong choose to take less
The weak give thanks for their fill
The strong give power to the weak
The weak give their support to the strong;
And they stand together as brothers
And so man prospers.

SILLY QUESTION

What if
we were meant to
love each other?

Survival, enemies;
bigger, stronger, fitter to better ridicule
and patronise the weak. I must win,
you must lose. You take
then I take, then you take, then …

What if
we were actually meant
to love each other?

"We're rich, you're pathetic. Statistics
show we're better. We can win races
and arguments and write history and tell better stories.
We're more beautiful. We speak
God's language. You speak funny.
We've got bigger bibles and bigger
bombs. We're blessed. You're corrupt
and ugly and Godless and stupid."

What if
we were actually meant
to love each other?

AFTER FREEDOM

Four slaves escape:

The first races to a distant city;
to indulge in choice.
The second boards a ship;
to make home amongst his roots.
The third cannot unslave himself;
so finds a new master.

The last escaped slave
returns,
with freedom in his eyes,
followed by an army.

BREAKFAST, 22 DECEMBER 2012

POET:

What do my eyes see?

Ramsay's Dunkirk?

Caesar and his hungry men?

Standing here on Dover's cliffs,

cliffs that remember so much,

so much white and crimson,

and so much of man struggling to find his place,

what do my eyes see?

FALSE PROPHET:

What do your eyes see?

POET:

They see wide blue-green ocean vistas

and distant muscular waves

that arrive below in giggles

as they dance upon pebbles,

countless pebbles,

that are still pebbles. I see

ecstatic gulls

that paint a thanksgiving prayer in the sky,

a clear, unbroken sky.

What do your eyes see?

FALSE PROPHET:
Mine saw that a gull
would deposit its droppings
on my head.
And now my eyes see
that one has just missed.

ROLIHLAHLA

In the final days

The Great Snake returned to the Garden

After ten thousand years of sin;

Rolihlahla was there,

As it had been written

Before the beginning.

Rolihlahla stood tall, a mighty warrior

Risen from mankind's cradle.

The Great Snake did not see him and slithered within reach of

    Rolihlahla's great foot –

The foot which held the hopes of souls through all time

But the great warrior did not lash out,

He did not crush the Snake's vile head,

That head which housed the spring of lies;

Instead he bent down to embrace the Great Snake;

Sensing the approach, the Snake struck, as lightning shot down

    into the Garden,

Sinking his fangs into Rolihlahla's chest,

Ageing the hero tenfold;

The Snake spat in his face

Striking him blind.

Time raced forward,

Graves grew deeper,

Humanity shrunk

And the earth stopped, forgetting how to do everything it had
    done for millenia. Darkness

Fell.

Rolihlahla spoke –

With a lilting melody

In a voice barely audible:

You and I are one

We are one song

We are one sound

You and I are the same

We are the same ocean

We are the same droplet

You and I are one

The Snake did not understand

Confused, it wedged its head under the heel of Rolihlahla's great
    foot.

Again Rolihlahla did not crush the Snake's head.

Again he spoke:

You and I are one

We are one song

We are one sound

You and I are the same
We are the same ocean
We are the same droplet

You and I are one

And now the Snake understood,
All of mankind and all of nature understood,
And light and life returned
In great abundance,
As it had been written
Before the beginning.

ABOUT THE AUTHOR

AE BALLAKISTEN published his first book of poetry, HEAP OF STONES, in 2009. At the age of 40, he retired from business to focus on his writing and social development in South Africa.

He holds degrees from University of London, University of the Witwatersrand and MIT. He has been admitted to Harvard where he will focus on public policy and social enterprise innovation.

He lives in Johannesburg with his wife, Taryn, and 8,000 books.